The Sonnet Remix

Creating Your Own Sonnets

The Sonnet Remix

Creating Your Own Sonnets

by

Eddie Morales

Contents

The Sonnet Remix

Creating Your Own Sonnets

The Origin of the Sonnet

The person credited with the creation of the first sonnet form is Giacomo Da Lentini, also called Jacopo Da Lentini, a Sicilian poet of the 13th century. He was a senior poet of the Sicilian school during the reign of the Holy Roman emperor Frederick II. He was considered a master by the poets of the following generation, including Dante, who memorialized him in his work the *Purgatorio*. None of his poetry survives in the original Sicilian dialect. Lentini's sonnet is very simple and uses very few rhymes, using the rhyme scheme abbaabbaabbacc.

In the 14th century, another Italian poet created another sonnet form. His name was Francesco Petrarca, commonly known as Petrarch (July 20, 1304 – July 19, 1374). Petrarch's sonnets grew in popularity and was imitated throughout Europe during the Renaissance. The rhyme scheme abbaabbacdecde then became the Italian or Petrarchan sonnet.

Moving forward, the sonnet form arrived in Spain during the early 15th century. The Spanish poets were mainly influenced by Petrarch's sonnets and with a little variation, the form was made popular by poets such as Francisco De Quevedo, Iñigo López de Mendoza, Lope de la Vega, and many others. With the Spanish sonnet you have two quatrains followed by two tercets, and the rhyme scheme is as follows, abba abba cdc dcd.

Later, in the 16th century, William Shakespeare (April 26, 1564 – April 23, 1616) changed the form and made it popular in England. The Shakespearean or English sonnet uses the rhyme scheme ababcdcdefefgg. It allows for more flexibility when considering the rhymes.

During Shakespeare's lifetime, another English poet devised his own rhyme scheme. His name was Sir Edmund Spenser (ca. 1552/1553 – January 13, 1599) and he created the Spenserian sonnet. His rhyme scheme is a bit difficult, although not as difficult as the sonnet Lentini created when it comes to finding words to rhyme. The rhyme scheme, ababbcbccdcdee identifies the Spenserian sonnet.

For centuries these sonnet forms have existed with little or no variation. For me, personally, if I were to consider the rhyming forms royalty, I consider the sonnet to be the king of all the poetic forms. There is something regal about the sonnet that draws me to it, and I never get tired of using this rhyming form. No matter in what other form I write in, sooner or later, I go back to the sonnet. I feel the more I master the sonnet, the more I master the other forms of rhyming poetry.

The Definition of a Sonnet

There are really only three requirements for a rhyming form to be defined as a sonnet. If you look at the sonnets mentioned, and read examples of each, you will notice that the sonnets have two things in common, and one thing that sets each apart.

The two things the sonnets have in common are the *fourteen lines* and the *iambic pentameter* meter (which is ten syllables per line). Anytime you see these two elements together in a poem, you can be pretty sure it is a sonnet. You then have to look at the one element that sets them apart, and that is the rhyme scheme.

If you examine the poem and see that the poem has the rhyme scheme ababcdcdefefgg, you are surely reading a Shakespearean or English sonnet. If your poem has the rhyme scheme abbaabbacdecde, you have a Petrarchan or Italian sonnet. The same goes for the Lentini, Spenserian and Spanish sonnets. The rhyme scheme identifies the origin of the poem. These three elements give you the sonnet.

Later on, I will be discussing variations of these sonnets. To keep them in order, I have devised a system to make them easy to understand. The sonnets mentioned up to now I will consider the Proper Sonnets. Any variations will have specific names which identifies the sonnet. This is where the *remixing* comes in.

The Sonnet Remix

The question now is what is a sonnet remix? It is a term I use, borrowed from the music industry, where an alternative version of a recorded song is made from an original version.

It is basically the adoption, alteration, and/or recombination of existing art forms, like sculpture, literature, paintings, etc., to create something new. Maybe, even take something old and modernize it; or at least, make it more appealing and interesting, as well as add some variety to the form. I thought, since I often write sonnets, it would be nice to find some way to make the sonnet more interesting.

However, before we can get to the remixing of this form, we must also take a look at the various stanzaic forms, because, as it turns out, the sonnet is really a derivative of the many different stanzas that exist, in one combination or another. We will also look at meter. After we do so, we will go about the task of modernizing this majestic of all poetic forms.

In addition, if only to be thorough, I will present the different *feet* used in poetry. A *foot* tells you whether or not you have a two-syllable or three-syllable word stressed in a certain way, depending on the name of the foot. For example, if you are using *iambic pentameter*, you are using five feet, with each foot having two syllables, with the second syllable being stressed, as in *ta-DUM*. More on this later.

The Proper Sonnets Side by Side

Before we proceed, let's take a look at the Proper Sonnets side by side so you can easily refer to them when you want to compare them to the sonnets we will create later on or you want a visual look at the original sonnet.

Lentinian	Petrarchan	Spanish	Spenserian	Shakespearean
a	a	a	a	a
b	b	b	b	b
b	b	b	a	a
a	a	a	b	b
a	a	a	b	c
b	b	b	c	d
b	b	b	b	c
a	a	a	c	d
a	c	c	c	e
b	d	d	d	f
b	e	c	d	e
a	c	d	c	f
c	d	c	e	g
c	e	d	e	g

From these sonnets many more sonnets will be created.

The Stanzaic Forms

The stanzaic forms are the building blocks of all rhyming poetry. Even the major Proper Sonnets are made up of two or more stanzaic forms and you can sequence any number of stanzas, but we are going to adhere to the three elements that define the sonnet, which are the fourteen lines, iambic pentameter, and rhyme scheme.

<u>List of Stanzaic Forms</u>

1) Couplet—two lines or Distich
2) Tercet—three lines
3) Quatrain—four lines
4) Quintet—five lines
5) Sestet—six lines or Hexastich
6) Septet—seven lines
7) Octet—eight lines
8) Nonet—nine lines
9) Decastich—ten lines
10) Eleven-line stanza
11) Duodecet—twelve lines
12) Thirteen-line stanza
13) Double-septet—14 lines

Things are about to shape up. The list can go on and on, but since we are going to adhere to the sonnet's definition of fourteen lines, no more stanzaic forms will be required. As you will see, these are more than enough for remixing the sonnet. Now, let's take a look at meter.

Meter

Poetic lines, otherwise known as verses, are classified according to the number of feet in a line. One foot is comprised of two or three syllables, depending on the name of the foot. See the table below:

FOOT	ACCENT	METER	SYL
Iambus	u / S	Iambic	2
Trochee	S / u	Trochaic	2
Spondee	S / S	Spondee	2
Pyrrhic	u / u	Pyrrhic	2
Anapest	u / u / S	Anapestic	3
Dactyl	S / u / u	Dactylic	3
Amphibrach	u / S / u	Amphibrach	3

(u=Unstressed; S=Stressed; Syl=Syllables)

If we use the iambus as an example, a verse containing a single foot is called a *monometer*. Below is a list of meters we will be concerned with:

1) Monometer
2) Dimeter
3) Trimeter
4) Tetrameter
5) Pentameter
6) Hexameter
7) Heptameter
8) Octameter

The number of feet in a line of English verse rarely exceeds eight, but it is possible for verses to contain more than eight but because eight is pretty much the maximum number of feet that can easily fit across the page, we will make eight feet our maximum.

The best known and most used foot in English verse is the iambus, which is used in conjunction with the pentameter meter, as in *iambic pentameter*. Poe used octameter lines in his famous poem, *The Raven*.

We now have enough knowledge of the form to create as many different sonnets as we can imagine. To the main four Proper Sonnets, leaving out Lentini's sonnet since it is not used any more, we are going to add at least ten more.

We will add still more later on as we use our building blocks of poetry to expand our knowledge of this rhyming form, but let us begin with the first building block, the *couplet*.

The Couplet Sonnet

The couplet, or *distich*, is the simplest of all stanzas, and contains two rhyming lines. Usually, the couplet is used for epigrams, as in the following:

When I am dead, I hope it may be said,
His sins were scarlet, but his books were read.
—Hilaire Belloc

If we use seven couplets together, you have, what I call, a *Proper Couplet Sonnet*. The couplet sonnet rhyme scheme would be as follows:

Couplet Sonnet
a-a-b-b-c-c-d-d-e-e-f-f-g-g

Look familiar? It should. It is the rhyme scheme to the English sonnet if you alternate the first twelve letters instead. So, the Shakespearean sonnet and this couplet sonnet are related.

The word *proper* in *Proper Couplet Sonnet* should tell you that we are adhering to the three requirements of a sonnet: fourteen lines, iambic pentameter meter, and the *couplet* identifies the form, in the same manner that the rhyme scheme ababcdcdefefgg identifies the sonnet as Shakespearean or English.

And why not?

There are no rules that say it can't be so.

The Tercet Sonnet

Now, let's follow the previous train of thought by next looking at the *tercet*. The tercet, or triplet, is three lines, and can be expressed as follows:

a-a-a or a-a-b or a-b-b or a-b-a or b-a-a

Usually the tercet uses *a-a-a* as the rhyme scheme, so I will use this rhyme scheme to create, if you follow me so far, the *Proper Tercet Sonnet* in this manner:

Proper Tercet Sonnet
a-a-a-b-b-b-c-c-c-d-d-d-e-e

That's four tercets followed by a couplet. Now the building blocks are starting to fall into place. Variations of the tercet sonnet can be:

a-a-b-c-c-d-e-e-f-g-g-h-i-i	or
a-a-b-c-c-b-e-e-b-g-g-b-i-i	or
a-b-b-c-d-d-e-f-f-g-h-h-i-i	or
a-b-b-a-c-c-a-d-d-a-e-e-f-f	or
a-b-a-c-d-c-e-f-e-g-h-g-i-i	or
a-b-a-c-b-c-d-b-d-e-b-e-f-f	

So far, we've added the Couplet Sonnet, the Tercet Sonnet, and six variations of the Tercet Sonnet to the four proper sonnets, and all meet the definition of a sonnet.

The Quatrain Sonnet

By now I'm sure you've figured out I'm going to create the *Proper Quatrain Sonnet.* William Shakespeare's and Sir Edmund Spenser's sonnets can be considered quatrain sonnets because they can be divided into three quatrains followed by a couplet. The same can be said for the Italian and Spanish sonnets with two quatrains followed by two tercets. You can also say they are *octaves* followed by *sestets,* but we'll get to that later.

Now, let's create a new *quatrain* sonnet. Since Shakespeare used the a-b-a-b quatrain and Petrarch used the a-b-b-a quatrain, I want to merge the two, and so as to visually see the process, I will place the English and Italian sonnets directly below the quatrain sonnet so you can see the similarities and differences.

Proper Quatrain Sonnets
a-b-a-b-c-d-d-c-e-f-e-f-g-g or
a-b-b-a-c-d-d c e f f e g-g

a-b-b-a-a-b-b-a-c-d-e-c-d-e (Italian)
a-b-a-b-c-d-c-d-e-f-e-f-g-g (English)

Of course, there are numerous variations of sonnets that can be made from the quatrain stanza. Here I used the English sonnet format for the first and third quatrain, and used the Italian sonnet format for the second quatrain, all the while adhering to the three simple requirements for a sonnet.

The Quintet Sonnet

Possible arrangements of the five-line stanza are even more numerous than for any of the stanzas previously mentioned. Usually, this stanza is a varied combination of couplets and triplets, and in many cases, quatrains with a single unrhymed line included, such as *a-b-a-b-c* or *a-b-b-a-c*, etc.

You can also use the two to three rhyming method and get variations like *a-a-b-b-b* or *a-b-b-a-a* or *a-b-b-b-a*, etc. Sonnets can be made from any one of these used together.

Put two such quintets together, add a couple of couplets or a quatrain at the end, and you have yourself a quintet sonnet. So, let's create a standard, proper quintet sonnet.

There are three basic ones, for example:

Quintet Sonnet
a-b-a-b-a-c-d-c-d-c-e-f-f-e   or
a-b-a-b-a-c-d-c-d-c-e-e-f-f   or
a-b-a-b-a-c-d-c-d-c-e-f-e-f

From these three, many more can be created, such as *a-b-a-b-c-d-e-d-e-c-f-g-f-g*, etc.

If you're like me and like to use a couplet at the end of a sonnet, you can use a-b-a-b-c-d-e-d-e-c-f-f-g-g.

Experiment, and put the sonnet together any way you like.

The Sestet Sonnet

The building blocks of sonnets are stacking up and many more variations can be created. This six-line stanza has various combinations of the couplet, triplet, and quatrain. A couplet and a quatrain can form a sestet. Three couplets can form a sestet. Two triplets can form a sestet.

If you take a look at a Petrarchan sonnet, you'll notice it closes with a sestet, usually with a rhyme scheme of, *a-b-c-a-b-c.* There are so many combinations. This is a stanza which makes it easy to create a sestet sonnet because by simply putting two sestets together and adding a couplet you have a sonnet.

Some six-line sestets can be:

a-a-b-b-c-c   a-b-b-a-c-c
a-a-b-c-c-b   a-a-a-b-b-b

There are many more, but this is the one I prefer for my *Proper Sestet Sonnet.*

Sestet Sonnet
a-b-c-a-b-c-d-e-f-d-e-f-g-g

I always look to create a sonnet that gives me the most varied rhymes. Using a rhyme scheme that has too few rhymes, like a-a-a-b-b-b-a-a-a-b-b-b-c-c is too limiting, but it is entirely up to the poet which rhyme scheme to choose.

13

The Septet, Octet, Nine-line Stanzas

The Rime Royal, or Rhyme Royal stanza consists of seven lines, usually in iambic pentameter. The rhyme scheme a-b-a-b-b-c-c was the standard narrative meter in the middle ages, and was introduced into English by Geoffrey Chaucer. Sir Edmund Spenser as well as Shakespeare used the form. This seven-line stanza makes creating a sonnet from it very easy. Simply put two rhyme royal stanzas together and you get:

Septet Sonnet (or Rhyme Royal Sonnet)

a-b-a-b-b-c-c-d-e-d-e-e-f-f

This is the basic septet sonnet and you can create other sonnets from the myriad of variations available from this form.

The Octave

The three basic building blocks of rhyming verse keep showing up, the couplet, triplet, and quatrain. What we discussed about the *Quatrain Sonnet* pretty much applies here. This eight-line stanza with its great number of combinations has been used by some poet at one time or another.

The four major sonnets are related to this stanza, especially the Petrarchan sonnet with its detached octave and rhyme scheme of a-b-b-a-a-b-b-a. So, any *quatrain sonnet* you create can also be considered an octet or *octave sonnet* and the same examples of the quatrain sonnet apply here. Also, maybe this: a-a-a-a-b-b-b-b-c-c-c-c-d-d.

The Nine-line Stanza

The nine-line stanza (from *New Rhyming Dictionary and Poets' Handbook* by Burges Johnson) has so many possibilities. The most noted form is that used by Spenser. Its rhyme scheme is: a-b-a-b-b-c-b-c-c and is exacting and usually written in iambic pentameter lines. The last line of the stanza contains twelve syllables and is called the Alexandrine, and ends the stanza with a finish that is rich and distinctive. The Spenserian stanza has been used in many noted English poems. Now, if we add a triplet and an ending couplet, you have the following:

> Nine-Line Stanza Sonnet
> a-b-a-b-b-c-b-c-c-d-d-d-e-e
> a-b-a-b-b-c-b-c-c-d-c-d-e-e (Spenserian sonnet)

I used the Spenserian form to create the sonnet, but you can use any variation of the nine-line stanza you want.

Here you can put your creativity to work. If you notice, there is only a one letter difference between the two sonnets. However, if you vary the rhyme scheme in the nine-line portion, you can create a sonnet totally different from these two sonnets.

From here on we don't need to discuss the other stanzaic forms (Decastich, eleven-line, Duodecet, thirteen-line, and fourteen-line). They would simply be an exercise to practice your ingenuity. Anything you can come up with for these stanzaic forms you probably will have already discovered in the previous stanzaic forms. It's all about the combinations of couplets, triplets, and quatrains.

The Puerto Rican Sonnet

This is a sonnet of my own creation.

There exists in Puerto Rico a song form called the *Décima*. It consists of four ten-line stanzas with tetrameter lines. The first stanza sets the rule. The rule is the last line of the first stanza must be repeated verbatim as the last line of each subsequent stanza. So, using capital C to mean the repeated line, the four stanzas go as follows:

1st stanza:	a-b-b-a-a-c-c-d-d-C
2nd stanza:	e-f-f-e-e-c-c-g-g-C
3rd stanza:	h-i-i-h-h-c-c-j-j-C
4th stanza:	k-l-l-k-k-c-c-m-m-C

It is an exacting song to write, and singers usually challenge each other to a competition where the first singer sets the theme, making up a song on the spot, and the person challenged must respond, and make up a song to refute the challenger. The winner is determined by the audience, and the singer who gets applauded the loudest wins.

I figured if I use pentameter lines in the Décima, and follow the rhyme scheme I have outlined above for the four stanzas, I believe I have created a new Décima Form of verse in the English language.

Proceeding, I took the rhyme scheme of the first stanza and created a sonnet of my own. Firstly, I converted the meter from tetrameter to pentameter, to meet one of the three elements required for a sonnet. Secondly, I extended the ten-line stanza to fourteen lines and gave it a logical rhyme scheme based on the Décima's own rhyme scheme, and I came up with the following sonnet:

Puerto Rican Sonnet
a-b-b-a-a-c-c-d-d-c-c-e-e-c

Here is an example of the Puerto Rican sonnet form from my bilingual book of poetry, *The Sonnet of Puerto Rico: El Soneto Borincano*—

Gold in San Juan Bautista (1506)

a There must be evil in this substance gold,
b Which sets the eyes of every god ablaze,
b This kingly token, for the ones we praise,
a That stirs up passions in the young and old,
a But brings much fury for a thing so cold.
c From Hispaniola word has come once more,
c Of all the gods who've traveled here before,
d One named, Juan Ponce, sailed and found our land;
d And if his will is kinder than his hand,
c May Borikén be isle the gods adore.
c Agüeybaná, who yellow metal wore,
e Great Chief Taino, wise and spirit true,
e By Mother Atabey he dreamt and knew
c That even gods may birth a god of war.

This sonnet can be presented in the Spanish version as two quintets and a quatrain➔ abbaa ccddc ceec.

List of Proper Sonnets

We now have more than thirteen sonnet forms to work with if you factor in the variations of the tercet, quatrain, quintet, sestet, septet, octet, and nine-line stanzas used.

1)	English	a-b-a-b-c-d-c-d-e-f-e-f-g-g
2)	Italian	a-b-b-a-a-b-b-a-c-d-e-c-d-e
3)	Spenserian	a-b-a-b-b-c-b-c-c-d-c-d-e-e
4)	Spanish	a-b-b-a-a-b-b-a-c-d-c-d-c-d
5)	Couplet	a-a-b-b-c-c-d-d-e-e-f-f-g-g
6)	Tercet	a-a-a-b-b-b-c-c-c-d-d-d-e-e
7)	Quatrain	a-b-b-a-c-d-d-c-e-f-f-e-g-g
8)	Quintet	a-b-a-b-a-c-d-c-d-c-e-f-f-e
9)	Sestet	a-b-c-a-b-c-d-e-f-d-e-f-g-g
10)	Septet	a-b-a-b-b-c-c-d-e-d-e-e-f-f
11)	Octet	a-a-a-a-b-b-b-b-c-c-c-c-d-d
12)	Nonet	a-b-a-b-b-c-b-c-c-d-d-d-e-e
13)	P.R.	a-b-b-a-a-c-c-d-d-c-c-e-e-c

You can use this chart as a quick reference guide when deciding what type of sonnet to write or to identify a specific rhyme scheme.

Meter Revisited

On page eight, I listed the eight meters that will be used to create more sonnets. They are monometer, dimeter, trimeter, tetrameter, pentameter, hexameter, heptameter, and octameter.

Apply these meters to the proper sonnets and the number of sonnets created is tremendous. If we look at the nomenclature there is a logical progression. However, in order to do this, we must look again at the requirements of a proper sonnet.

A proper sonnet has fourteen lines, is in iambic pentameter, and has a rhyme scheme that identifies the sonnet. The Shakespearean sonnet has these three elements, and I will use it to create a naming process for all of the sonnets you can create from it.

If we adjust one of the elements, for example, the meter, doesn't the fourteen lines and the rhyme scheme still give you a sonnet? I believe so. See below.

Metered Stanzaic Nomenclature

1) Monometer Shakespearean sonnet
2) Dimeter Shakespearean sonnet
3) Trimeter Shakespearean sonnet
4) Tetrameter Shakespearean sonnet
5) Pentameter Shakespearean sonnet (standard)
6) Hexameter Shakespearean sonnet
7) Heptameter Shakespearean sonnet
8) Octometer Shakespearean sonnet

If you keep the fourteen lines and follow the rhyme scheme of an English or Shakespearean sonnet, you still have a sonnet. At least, if we modernize our definition of the sonnet form, it will be so. This modernization, or remixing as I call it, is what gives the sonnet form a new face, and renewed life.

Now we can take all of those sonnets created earlier and add a new dimension. You can now create a

Shakespearean Tetrametric sonnet or a

Petrarchan Trimetric sonnet, etc.

Other Types of Sonnets

Occitan Sonnet

The sole confirmed surviving sonnet in the Occitan language is confidently dated to 1284, and is conserved only in troubadour manuscript *P*, an Italian *chansonnier* of 1310, now XLI.42 in the Biblioteca Laurenziana in Florence. It was written by Paolo Lanfranchi da Pistoia and is addressed to Peter III of Aragon. (Wikipedia). It employs the rhyme scheme a-b-a-b-a-b-a-b-c-d-c-d-c-d.

This should look familiar

Occitan Sonnet
a-b-a-b-a-b-a-b-c-d-c-d-c-d
a-b-b-a-a-b-b-a-c-d-c-d-c-d (Spanish)

In the course of creating your sonnets, you may have constructed an Occitan sonnet using the couplets, triplets, quatrains, and sestets. Here we have two quatrains and a sestet.

Inverted Sonnet

Want to create more sonnets? Take a sonnet that ends in a couplet and write the couplet as the first two lines of the poem, then finish the poem by using the rest of the sonnet form.

a-b-a-b-c-d-c-d-e-f-e-f-g-g (English)
a-a-b-c-b-c-d-e-d-e-f-g-f-g (Inverted English)

Crown of Sonnets

A *crown of sonnets* or *sonnet corona* is a sequence of sonnets, usually addressed to one person, and/or concerned with a single theme. Each of the sonnets explores one aspect of the theme, and is linked to the preceding and succeeding sonnets by repeating the final line of the preceding sonnet as its first line. The first line of the first sonnet is repeated as the final line of the final sonnet, thereby bringing the sequence to a close.

Sonnet Cycle

A sonnet cycle is a group of sonnets arranged to address a particular person or theme, and designed to be read both as a collection of fully realized individual poems and as a single poetic work comprising all the individual sonnets.

A sonnet cycle may have any theme, but unrequited love is the most common. The arrangement of the sonnets generally reflects thematic concerns, with chronological arrangements (whether linear, like a progression, or cyclical, like the seasons) being the most common. A sonnet cycle may also have allegorical or argumentative structures which replace or complement chronology.

While the thematic arrangement may reflect the unfolding of real or fictional events, the sonnet cycle is very rarely narrative; the narrative elements may be inferred, but provide background structure, and are never the primary concern of the poet's art.

Sonnet Sequence

A sonnet sequence is a group of sonnets unified thematically to create a long work, although generally, unlike the stanza, each sonnet so connected can also be read as a meaningful separate unit.

The sonnet sequence was a very popular genre during the Renaissance, following the pattern of Petrarch.

Sonnet sequences are typically closely based on Petrarch, either closely emulating his example or working against it. The subject is usually the speaker's unhappy love for a distant beloved, following the courtly love tradition of the troubadours from whom the genre ultimately derived.

An exception is Edmund Spenser's *Amoretti,* where the wooing is successful, and the sequence ends with an *Epithalamion*, a marriage song.

Heroic Crown

An advanced form of crown of sonnets is also called a *sonnet redoublé* or *heroic crown*, comprising fifteen sonnets, in which the sonnets are linked as described above, but the final binding sonnet is made up of all the first lines of the preceding fourteen, in order. The poem in my book, *The Burning of Bishop Nicholas Ridley*, is a Heroic Crown.

Fourteener

A line consisting of fourteen syllables, usually having seven *iambic heptametric* feet, most commonly found in English poetry produced in the 16th and 17th centuries, also a *quatorzain*, from the French *quatorze* meaning fourteen.

Quatorzain

A poem of fourteen lines. Historically the term has often been used interchangeably with the term *sonnet*. Various writers have tried to draw distinctions between 'true' sonnets, and quatorzains. Nowadays the term is seldom used, and when it is, it usually is used to distinguish fourteen-line poems that do not follow the various rules that describe the sonnet.

Dante's Variation

Most Sonnets in Dante's *La Vita Nuova* are Petrarchan, but some are not. Chapter VII gives sonnet *O voi che per la via*, with two sestets (AABAAB AABAAB) and two quatrains (CDDC CDDC), and Ch. VIII, *Morte villana*, with two sestets (AABBBA AABBBA) and two quatrains (CDDC CDDC).

If we adhere to the strict definition of a sonnet, we need to make an adjustment to Dante's Variation Sonnet. The task is simple. Using Dante's sestets, we can create two separate 14-line versions of this sonnet form by adding a couplet to the two sestets as follows:

Dante's Sonnet
a-a-b-a-a-b-a-a-b-a-a-b-c-c
a-a-b-b-b-a-a-a-b-b-b-a-c-c

Caudate Sonnet

A caudate is an expanded version of the sonnet. It consists of 14 lines in standard sonnet forms followed by a *coda* (Latin *cauda* meaning "tail", from which the name is derived). The invention of this sonnet form is credited to Francesco Berni. According to the *Princeton Encyclopedia of Poetry,* the form is most frequently used for satire, such as the most prominent English instance, Milton's *On the New Forcers of Conscience Under the Long Parliament.* An example could be:

a-b-a-b-c-d-c-d-e-f-e-f-g-g h-i-h-i

Here, you have an English sonnet plus a quatrain. Use the couplet, tercet, quatrain, etc., to create other caudate sonnets.

Curtal Sonnet

The Curtal sonnet is a curtailed or contracted sonnet. It refers specifically to a sonnet made up of 11 lines rhyming *abcabc dcbdc* or *abcabc dbcdc* with the last line a tail, or half a line. The term was used by the poet Gerard Manley Hopkins to describe the form that he used in such poems as "Pied Beauty" and "Peace." *Curtal* is now an obsolete word meaning "shortened." (Encyclopedia Britannica).

Since I want to adhere to the fourteen-line versions of the sonnet, as per the definition, this form is presented for information only. It is not considered a true sonnet.

Pushkin Sonnet

This form was popularized (or invented) by the Russian poet Alexander Pushkin, through his novel in verse *Eugene Onegin*. The work was mostly written in verses of *iambic tetrameter* with the rhyme scheme:

aBaBccDDeFFeGG

The lowercase letters represent feminine endings (i.e., with an additional unstressed syllable) and the uppercase representing masculine ending (i.e. stressed on the final syllable).

Unlike other traditional forms, such as the Petrarchan sonnet or Shakespearean sonnet, the Onegin stanza does not divide into smaller stanzas of four lines or two in an obvious way.

There are many different ways the sonnet can be divided: for example, the first four lines can form a quatrain, or instead join with the "cc" to form a set. The form's flexibility allows the author more scope to change how the semantic sections are divided from sonnet to sonnet, while keeping the sense of unity provided by following a fixed rhyme scheme.

Also, being written in *iambic tetrameter* imparts a stronger sense of motion than other sonnets, which use the more common *iambic pentameter*. Although this may be the case, I still want to adhere to the definition of a sonnet, and the Pushkin Sonnet in iambic pentameter I would consider as the Proper Pushkin sonnet.

NOTE: After coming up with my nomenclature for the sonnets, I did a little research, starting with the English Monometer Sonnet and I looked up one-word sonnets.

What is a word sonnet?

It is a new variation of the traditional form, fourteen lines long, but with only one word set for each verse. Concise and usually visual in effect, this miniature version can contain one or more sentences, as the articulation requires.

The earliest word sonnet seems to have seen the light of print approximately twenty years ago. In 1985, the American poet Brad Leithauser introduced a monosyllabic ironic poem entitled "Post-Coitum Tristesse" that was later included in a volume of his work and the anthology of New Formalist poetry, *Rebel Angels*. One of a kind, Leithauser's word sonnets perhaps set a precedent for others to follow.

If Leithauser wrote a one-word sonnet in 1985, then I'm not the only one trying to modernize the form.

Modernizing the Sonnet

We now have over forty sonnet forms at our disposal, but how do we modernize them? The answer is so simple that I can't really say I discovered it. Somebody else must have. All you need to do is to dispense with the line length while keeping the fourteen lines and rhyme scheme of the different sonnets intact. Take all of the proper forms (the old forms as well as the new ones created here) and vary the line lengths. Write one of each, and you'll end up with so many poems you won't know what to do with them all. Well, maybe publish your own book.

Updated List of Sonnets

1) English a-b-a-b-c-d-c-d-e-f-e-f-g-g
   - Monometer
   - Dimeter
   - Trimeter
   - Tetrameter
   - Pentameter
   - Hexameter
   - Heptameter
   - Octameter
   - Caudate
   - Inverted (for couplet ending sonnets)
   - Modern
2) Spenserian   a-b-a-b-b-c-b-c-c-d-c-d-e-e
3) Italian   a-b-b-a-a-b-b-a-c-d-e-c-d-e
4) Spanish   a-b-b-a a-b-b-a c-d-c d-c-d
5) Couplet   a-a-b-b-c-c-d-d-e-e-f-f-g-g
6) Tercet   a-a-a-b-b-b-c-c-c-d-d-d-e-e
7) Quatrain   a-b-b-a-c-d-d-c-e-f-f-e-g-g
8) Quintet   a-b-a-b-a-c-d-c-d-c-e-e-f-f
9) Sestet   a-b-c-a-b-c-d-e-f-d-e-f-g-g
10) Septet   a-b-a-b-b-c-c-d-e-d-e-e-f-f
11) Nine-line   a-b-a-b-b-c-b-c-c-d-d-d-e-e
12) Occitan   a-b-a-b a-b-a-b c-d-c-d-c-d
13) P.R.   a-b-b-a-a-c-c-d-d-c-c-e-e-c
14) Dante's   a-a-b-b-b-a-a-a-b-b-b-a-c-c
15) Pushkin   a-B-a-B-c-c-D-D-e-F-F-e-G-G*

*Letters: LC=feminine UC=masculine rhyme ending

If you do the math, from the list of sonnets on the previous page, you have at least fifteen sonnet forms, and eleven ways to write each one! That means if you were to write one sonnet in each form, that's 165 different sonnets. That's enough for almost two 100-page (accounting for title page, dedication page, table of contents, etc.) books of poetry.

Examples of Stanzaic Sonnets

In the next several pages I have provided examples of sonnets using the different stanzaic forms I have earlier discussed so you can have a visual of what the sonnets look like. In some cases, I have used a slightly smaller font in order to get as much of the lines to fit correctly. On a standard sheet of paper, of course, they would fit neatly across the page, with octameter meter being the longest line you should use.

I believe good writing comes *after* the practice of writing, and in order to write good sonnets you have to practice writing them, hopefully getting better at it after writing many of your own.

After reading the *iambic octameter* sonnet I will present variations of the sonnets discussed and how the sonnet can be used in different ways.

As you can see, with a little modification of the standard definition of the sonnet, many more sonnets can be created. Below, I have mainly used the Shakespearean or English sonnet as an example, but you can use the other sonnet forms, like the Italian or Petrarchan, sonnet to create many more sonnets. Go ahead, experiment. Have fun trying.

Iambic Monometer

Adieu

I long
To sing
A song
Come spring.
But if
You leave
I'll live
To grieve.
My soul
Won't take
The hole
You'll make.
Say bye—
I die.

Iambic Dimeter

Don't Say Adieu

You know I long
To dance and sing
A waltz, a song,
With you come spring.
I won't forgive
You, should you leave.
For you I live—
You go, I'll grieve.
You know my soul
Can never take
The blackest hole
In me you'll make.
Don't say goodbye!
If so, I'll die.

Iambic Trimeter

Never Say Adieu

My love, you know I long
Have craved to dance and sing
Perchance a waltz, a song,
Like lovers do in spring.
Know well I won't forgive
You ever, should you leave.
Tis known for you I live—
So if you go, I'll grieve.
You surely know my soul
Can never ever take
The deepest, blackest hole
In me you'll truly make.
I beg, don't say goodbye!
If so, you'll see me die.

Iambic Tetrameter

Going Crazy

You say my belfry's lost a bat,
But really what you meant to say
Is that I've lost it, that is that,
Or lost my marbles in some way.
But maybe what you say is true,
I may just have a screw that's loose,
And if I listen more to you,
I'll turn more like a silly goose.
You drive me nuts, you nagging loon,
I cannot take much more of this.
Please let me play the dumb buffoon,
Let crazy do as crazy is.
Of all the things that I have lost
I truly miss my mind the most.

Iambic Pentameter

(Standard Shakespearean Sonnet)

Love is Everything

Whatever sustenance I get from food
Or drink, or comfort I obtain against
The rain, or lifelines grasped to do me good,
And so on, none compare to love incensed
By its own need to give itself away,
Or be received without condition or
Restraint; yes, lack of this affective sway
May lead the bargain right to death's own door.
However, one by one, with love, I see
The saving grace that once may salvage all
Of what is life, and which I feel may be
The greatest, soothing comfort overall.
The flesh may eat and drink, stay well and dry,
But, without love, the soul is first to die.

(From my book *Poems for Edna*)

Iambic Hexameter

When My Pen Runs Out of Ink

The day my pen has shed the last of all its tears,
And every drop off ink upon the pages of
My book has dried—denied will not be those who love
The rhyming forms. These echoed words which bare my
years
And life may be the only proof I lived. My fears
and hopes which shaped the ink have driven me to move
Me to a higher plane of thought a step above
The normal grind of verse which never soothed my ears.
So take my verses, echoed as they are, extol
Them or condemn them, but do *something* either way.
My death will be your pass to judge them day by day,
Until some night, I hope, they're worth the time you spend
Reciting meager rhymes I *had* to write, and all
Of which, through diligence and sleepless nights, I penned.

Iambic Heptameter

Yours is the Face

Your face, my love, the countenance I've yearned too long
to see,
Is perfect for my eyes; it soothes my sight like drink for
thirst.
Now, other visages within my gaze are false to me,
And real's the dream, that in my nights, my soul has
nursed.
And here you are, a foreign land, which came to me
instead,
So I could travel little in my quest to find a place —
Where eyes can melt all winter ice and bosom rest my
head;
Where kisses cool and sear the same with heaven's blessed
grace.
You are the right to any wrong, which so far crossed my
heart,
And level path to rocky roads that steer a man astray.
You are the source of every seedling's hope to make a start;
You're honesty, and goodness, which will soothe me
through each day.
No longer need my eyes, though time detract, a better sight
Than this: your face — which gives me sun by day and
moon by night.

Iambic Octameter

Religiously Mathematical

It is but genius when it comes to all that math can offer me,
As sure as two plus two is added to make nothing else but
four;
And when it comes to multiplying, factoring the nth degree,
You calculate the time it takes the Milky Way to reach my
door.
Quadratically I may pursue binomial theorems to the end,
With interesting facts about the square of the hypotenuse,
While neutron stars and pulsars go on threatening us both,
my friend,
While new stars form to then replace the systems stars no
longer use.
The particle where God resides has Higgs all in a frenzied
state.
Where quarks, and mesons, bosons, and the like, all readily
prevail,
There must be God somewhere inside to tempt the hand of
fickle fate,
And prove there is a master plan to take all heretics to jail.
To find the answer to the question that mankind has always
asked,
I'll need to find that one equation that will leave my God
unmasked.

Couplet Sonnet

Trick or treat

It was a dark and stormy Halloween,
No children trick-or-treating could be seen.
They kept indoors where mischief could be hid,
Where candy waited for each demon kid.
A witch was baking cookie-kids galore,
First baking one and then a dozen more.
The wolfman waited for the rain to stop,
To eat the children at the candy shop.
With devil's candied apples, poison filled,
The Devil has a dozen neighbors killed.
The ghouls were hungry, fit then to be tied,
But well the treaters all remained inside.
If ever there was ever good this day,
I made this up and no one's died today.

Tercet Sonnet

Of Stars and Dreams

The stars hang twinkling in the summer sky
Presenting each a sparkling sensual eye,
But, by your beauty, jealously they cry.
Oh, green becomes the envious silver moon,
With icy moonbeams helter-skelter strewn,
Like dizzy fireflies act in nights of June.
Come let your loving arms share my embrace;
Let lips on lips be always ours to grace;
Our bodies lying on sheer silk and lace.
Let's give our passion's candle needed fire,
To blend our dancing shadows with desire
And climb our sacred passion ever higher.
And once we've made of summer night the most,
I'll meet you in some dream where eyes are lost.

Quatrain Sonnet

Brightest Light

Reveal your thoughts to me my blushing Rose.
What jealousy conspires to lose your face?
What envy threatens, Lily, lose your Grace?
Why does the Orchid's face look so morose?
Why, Sun, do all your rays so sadly shine?
I know! She has the fire that brightest burns
Where every creature's head in wonder turns
To beauty which is heavenly divine.
O fickle Destiny, don't brood this way,
With vain attempts to bring me gloom.
The Daisy is no lesser for her bloom,
Though to another I gave heart away.
The Tulips bless, wherever they may grow,
And bless the woman whom I've grown to know.

In this *quatrain sonnet* I used neither the rhyme scheme a-b-a-b-c-d-c-d-e-f-e-f-g-g of the Shakespearean sonnet nor the rhyme scheme a-b-b-a-a-b-b-a-c-d-e-c-d-e of the Petrarchan sonnet. However, if you notice, it is more of a variation of the Shakespearean sonnet than it is of the Petrarchan sonnet even though it starts out like a Petrarchan sonnet. Still, if you wanted to, you could end it like a Petrarchan sonnet with a-b-b-a-c-d-d-c-e-f-g-e-f-g.

The Quintet Sonnet

This unique sonnet offers an opportunity to use a couplet in the beginning followed by two quintets and also ending it with a couplet, as follows:

a-a-b-c-b-c-b-d-e-d-e-d-f-f

It's All About the Dash

No matter what the length a life may fill
For sure a death is even longer still.
A stillbirth may just end it right away
Before a soul knows even what life is,
And in this tragic game of life we play,
Unfortunate are they who know not bliss,
The joy of life, but breathless, lose the way.
But those who breathe at birth have little time,
To make of life what little they can make.
So much depends on reason and on rhyme,
And on the different paths the flesh may take,
Where tragic life may be, or life sublime.
Two dates upon your headstone will be writ,
And you have but the dash to make the best of it.

Here I decided to use as Alexandrine in the last line just to vary the ending couplet from the beginning couplet.

The Sestet Sonnet

Try writing a sonnet using two sestets followed by a couplet. You can use any variation of the sestet you want, for example in the following rhyme scheme:

a-b-a-b-a-b-c-d-c-d-c-d-e-e

The Septet Sonnet

This one is easy since it calls for two seven-line stanzas. Try using: a-b-c-a-b-c-b-d-e-f-d-e-f-f.

The Octet Sonnet

Use for starters a-b-c-d-a-b-c-d-e-f-g-e-f-g where the sestet is like that of the Petrarchan sonnet.

Let the Remixing Continue

Let us use the following poem to see how a sonnet can be used in conjunction with other forms:

Upon Reading Youth and Age by S T C

Immortal was my mind and body fit,
Invincibly my form did take the world,
When wooing let me make the best of it,
And conquering, my strength was there unfurled,
When I was young!
The summer heat could not my fury quell,
Nor Winter's breath take loving from my hips.
My words could ladies make to swoon a spell,
For virile was my back when muscle rips,
When I was young and felt much like a god,
In times when steely thighs and viselike hands,
And straightness of my spine matched youth's façade,
To render me all things that Life commands.
There were no paths too dangerous to take,
Where wingless still I flew among the stars,
Where fearlessly my sojourns I did make,
No matter low or high were set the bars.
But now is now and that was way back when
Bold Difference came between my Now and Then.
Ah, to think that I was young!
Six decades has my life so swiftly run,
And being in the race, the finish line
Runs towards me, pacing down the ticks of time,
Because this body's quickly in decline,
Unlike when I was young.
I'm cautious now of fearless wind and tide,

Where once the weather feared my lungs and breath.
But if my soul fears not the other side,
Again, immortal will I be upon my death.

In the poem above I have hidden a Shakespearean sonnet. If you refer back to a *caudate sonnet*, it is an expanded version of the sonnet. It consists of 14 lines in standard sonnet forms followed by a *coda* (Latin *cauda* meaning "tail", from which the name is derived).

Well in this poem I have not only added a *tail*, but a head as well. Below I have presented a visual.

Upon Reading Youth and Age by S T C
Immortal was my mind and body fit,
Invincibly my form did take the world,
When wooing let me make the best of it,
And conquering, my strength was there unfurled,
When I was young!

The summer heat could not my fury quell,
Nor Winter's breath take loving from my hips.
My words could ladies make to swoon a spell,
For virile was my back when muscle rips,
When I was young and felt much like a god,
In times when steely thighs and viselike hands,
And straightness of my spine matched youth's façade,
To render me all things that Life commands.
There were no paths too dangerous to take,
Where wingless still I flew among the stars,
Where fearlessly my sojourns I did make,
No matter low or high were set the bars.
But now is now and that was way back when
Bold Difference came between my Now and Then.

Ah, to think that I was young!
Six decades has my life so swiftly run,
And being in the race, the finish line
Runs towards me, pacing down the ticks of time,
Because this body's quickly in decline,
Unlike when I was young.

I'm cautious now of fearless wind and tide,
Where once the weather feared my lungs and breath.
But if my soul fears not the other side,
Again, immortal will I be upon my death.

(From my book *Too Much Wine Before Midnight*)

I'm sure you can see the sonnet now. I have placed
a quintet at the head of the sonnet, a sestet at the end of the
sonnet followed by an ending quatrain.

In this poem I have taken a Petrarchan, or Italian, sonnet and added a tail to make a *caudate* Petrarchan sonnet. I also decided to keep the fourteen lines as well as the rhyme scheme of the Italian sonnet but decided to not pay attention to the length of the lines.

Diamorphine Droop
(South Bronx circa 1966)

He's only fourteen, two years older than me!
Near the liquor store, sitting on the stoop,
He's gone, gone, gone in the droop,
Unable to hear, unable to see.
Got himself caught up in a shooting spree;
You can tell by the tracks on his arms, what a dupe.
The fire raging like a five-alarm, that's the scoop,
Raging, along the Heroin Sea.
His gums all black, teeth falling out, and damn skinny as well,
Looking like something the Devil spit out of hell,
But ask, and he'll tell you, with a drooling slur, "I'm doing fine."
That's if what you call fine is the same as whack,
In which case, he's in the smack
Pretty much all of the time.

So, the people treat him like any other bum!
And who the hell cares?
Folks have to tend to their own affairs,
Not to scum of the earth, filth deeper than scum.
Right?
But he's only fourteen! Somebody's son!
Then again, like I said, who the hell cares?

Now let's experiment. What if we take the Italian sonnet in the poem and present it in another way without using punctuation. It's what I call modernizing the sonnet, like so:

Diamorphine Droop
(South Bronx circa 1966)

He's only fourteen
Two years older than me
Near the liquor store sitting on the stoop
He is gone
Gone
Gone
In the droop
Unable to hear
Unable to see
Got himself caught up in a shooting spree
You can tell by the tracks on his arms
What a dupe
The fire raging like a five-alarm
That's the scoop
Raging
Along the Heroin Sea.
His gums are all black
Teeth falling out
Damn skinny as well,
Looking like some *thing* the Devil spit out of hell
But ask and he'll tell you
With a drooling slur I'm doing fine
That's if what you call fine is the same as whack
In which case he's in the smack
Pretty much all of the time

As you can see, the arrangement of the sonnet's lines presents a whole different dimension. It is still a Petrarchan sonnet but you would never know it by looking at the poem. How about the following Shakespearean sonnet?

Poor Boy Blues
(circa 1966)

Gangs and drugs, not my thing.
The whores on Hunts Point, not for me.
I'm trying to get inside my head, while they bring
The cops in on a killing spree;
So the cops hope, but all I want to do is cope.
Paddy wagon's standing by,
Looking out for money, guns, and dope.
There's nothing here, I don't want to die,
But, no use, the bullets hail;
Bullets, blue with badges, some corrupt,
If you're not dead, then jail,
Makes me feel like throwing up.
Shots! Shots over my head!
Somewhere, again, some momma's child lies dead.

The Shakespearean sonnet above has different line lengths but still maintains the fourteen lines and the rhyme scheme of this particular form. Now, we can take the same sonnet and modernize, as we did with the Petrarchan sonnet before and make it look like so:

Poor Boy Blues
(circa 1966)

Gangs and drugs
Not my thing
The whores on Hunts Point
Not for me
I'm trying to get inside my head
While they bring
The cops in on a killing spree
So the cops hope
But all I want to do is cope
Paddy wagon's standing by
Looking out for money
Guns
Dope
There's nothing here
I don't want to die
But, no use the bullets hail
Bullets
Blue with badges
Some corrupt
If you're not dead then jail
Makes me feel like throwing up
Shots
Shots over my head
Somewhere again
Some momma's child lies dead

I could have taken a standard or proper
Shakespearean sonnet and broken the lines in the same
manner and no one would be the wiser. It would still be a
Shakespearean sonnet, nevertheless.

How to Write a Sonnet

Everyone has their own way or their own technique for learning. I don't know if my method will work for you, but maybe it will. It's all about practice. If you want to be a good basketball player, you have to practice. You want to be the greatest, you have to practice the hardest. The same goes for writing a sonnet. You have to *practice* writing one in order to become great at writing one.

The simplest way to start is with one line. Start writing one line at a time and pay attention to the number of syllables in that line and make sure it is exactly ten syllables.

A dictionary will help by showing you how the word is broken up syllabically. It will also show you which syllable is accented. Keep writing one liners, again and again, for as long as it takes.

For this exercise, I'm going to use the most widely used foot, the *iamb*. The line will be in *iambic pentameter*. The syllables will be presented here with an unstressed syllable followed by a stressed syllable, and the iambic pentameter line looks as follows:

ta-DUM | ta-DUM | ta-DUM | ta-DUM | ta-DUM

This is the beat that will be used in creating a sonnet. The hard beat falls on the second, fourth, sixth, eighth, and tenth beat. Each *ta-DUM* is an iambic foot. Using an actual line from one of Shakespeare's sonnets, Sonnet 18, the line is as follows:

shall I | com-PARE | thee TO | a SUM | mer's DAY?

Write a line of your own and pay attention to see if the unstressed and stressed pattern is adhered to. Don't worry if the line makes any sense. This is all for practice.

Write one line, and then another, and so on. Practice at your own pace, until you're able to write an iambic pentameter line at will.

Once you have the ability to write any iambic pentameter line, go on to writing a couplet. Practice writing the couplet until that becomes second nature.

Once you have mastered writing iambic pentameter couplets, go on to writing a quatrain by using two couplets in one stanza. The couplet and the quatrain are the only two building blocks you will ever need to make a sonnet.

Once you have mastered the two-couplet quatrain, alternate the end rhyme. For example, if you want to write a Shakespearean sonnet, you want alternately rhyming lines, such as:

a-b-a-b

So now you start practicing writing a-b-a-b quatrains, until doing so becomes second nature. Follow this by writing two quatrains as follows:

a-b-a-b c-d-c-d

Logically, from here you go to three quatrains:

a-b-a-b c-d-c-d e-f-e-f

Since you've already practiced writing couplets, the ending of the sonnet becomes easier, and you then add the g-g couplet at the end.

Figure, let's say, in one year you want to be able to write sonnets. Set aside, at first, a few minutes each day, or so, to write single lines in iambic pentameter. Do this for the first month or two.

Then on the third and fourth month practice writing couplets.

On the fifth and sixth month write two-couplet quatrains.

On the seventh and eighth month switch from writing two-couplet quatrains to quatrains with alternately rhyming lines.

On the ninth and tenth month write your quatrain pairs, and then your quatrain trios.

By the time you get to the end of the twelfth month you're ready to add your ending couplet to the three quatrains you created, and you've finally written your sonnet.

THE END

Bibliography

- I. Bell, et al. *A Companion to Shakespeare's Sonnets*. Blackwell Publishing, 2006. ISBN 1-4051-2155-6.
- Bertoni, Giulio (1915). *I Trovatori d'Italia: Biografie, testi, tradizioni, note*. Rome: Società Multigrafica Editrice Somu.
- T. W. H. Crosland. *The English Sonnet*. Hesperides Press, 2006. ISBN 1-4067-9691-3.
- J. Fuller. *The Oxford Book of Sonnets*. Oxford University Press, 2002. ISBN 0-19-280389-1.
- J. Fuller. *The Sonnet*. (The Critical Idiom: #26). Methuen & Co., 1972. ISBN 0-416-65690-0.
- J. Hollander. *Sonnets: From Dante to the Present*. Everyman's Library, 2001. ISBN 0-375-41177-1.
- P. Levin. *The Penguin Book of the Sonnet: 500 Years of a Classic Tradition in English*. Penguin, 2001. ISBN 0-14-058929-5.
- S. Mayne. *Ricochet, Word Sonnets - Sonnets d'un mot*. Translated by Sabine Huynh. University of Ottawa Press, 2011. ISBN 978-2-7603-0761-2
- J. Phelan. *The Nineteenth Century Sonnet*. Palgrave Macmillan, 2005. ISBN 1-4039-3804-0.
- S. Regan. *The Sonnet*. Oxford University Press, 2006. ISBN 0-19-289307-6.
- M. R. G. Spiller. *The Development of the Sonnet: An Introduction*. Routledge, 1992. ISBN 0-415-08741-4.

M. R. G. Spiller. *The Sonnet Sequence: A Study of Its Strategies*. Twayne Pub., 1997. ISBN 0-8057-0970-3

OTHER BOOKS BY THE AUTHOR

A Reason for Rhyme
ISBN 978-0615566924

The Suicide Sonnets
ISBN 978-1467931281

Count Edweird Lefang's Rhymin' Halloween (Funny Cover)
ISBN 978-0615565163

Count Edweird Lefang's Rhymin' Halloween (Signature Cover)
ISBN 978-1938094019

A Candle on Fire
ISBN 978-1938094026

Poems for Edna
ISBN 978-1938094033

The Burning of Bishop Nicholas Ridley
ISBN 978-1938094040

For the Love of Nine Muses
ISBN 978-1938094057

The Sonnet of Puerto: El Soneto Borincano
ISBN 978-1938094002

Too Much Wine Before Midnight Not Enough Before Noon
ISBN 978-1-938094-07-1

The Whispers of Pow Chin Chew
ISBN 978-1-938094-08-8

www.poeticon.com